For My Dear Friend

Yours Sincerely

Dear Friend

Stacie Orrico
with
Melissa Riddle

J. Countryman
Nashville, Tennessee

Cover and Interior design: DeAnna Pierce, The Office of Bill Chiaravalle, Sisters, Oregon

Project Editor: Jenny Baumgartner, with special thanks to Julie Young and Kim Washam

ISBN: 0-8499-9546-9

Printed and bound in the United States of America

www.thomasnelson.com

This is a book. Paper and stitching and pictures and such. It cannot begin to contain all the things I know to be true of you, all the hope I have for you. But read it all the same. Listen to the music, and read it again. And if you still can't quite believe everything you've read, all you have to do is call me.

I'm here for you.

❖ Dear Friend ❖

Dear Friend, what's on your mind?
You don't laugh the way you used to, but I've noticed how you cry
Dear Friend, I feel so helpless
I see you sit in silence as you face the pain each day
I feel there's nothing I can do
I know you don't feel pretty even though you are
But it wasn't your beauty that found room in my heart
Dear Friend, you are so precious, dear friend
Dear Friend, I'm here for you
I know that you don't talk too much
But we can share this day anew
Dear Friend, please don't feel like you're alone
There is someone who is praying, praying for your peace of mind
Hoping joy is what you find
I know you don't feel weak even though you are
But it wasn't your strength that found room in my heart
Dear Friend, you are so precious, dear friend

*Dear Child, You're in my arms
I know that you feel swept aside, but you don't have to run and hide
Dear Child, I chose you as my beloved daughter

* UNRECORDED THIRD VERSE

Dear Friend,
What's on your mind?

You don't laugh the way you used to...

When joy flies away,

YOUR MIND TO MINE,

we were made to feel and to know where the laughter hides,

MY HEART TO YOURS.

how to awaken hope.

DOUBT, *fear*, SADNESS, OVERWHELMING *ache*.

they all stop by for a visit.
they settle in your favorite chair
and wear out the welcome they never got.

sometimes,
it takes a friend who knows the truth
to run them off.

Will you let me?

WE DON'T HAVE TO BE *brave*
if we have heart

* * *

WE DON'T HAVE TO BE *calm*
when the waters are rising

* * *

WE DON'T HAVE TO BE *silent.*
a silent scream is still a scream

AND A *silent*
PRAYER
IS *still*
A PRAYER.

Don't be CONFUSED,
don't be AFRAID,
EVERYTHING PASSES
GOD DOES NOT CHANGE.
Patience wins every time.
And if you have God, you lack nothing
GOD ALONE IS ENOUGH.

TERESA OF AVILA, PARAPHRASED

And there's me

I COME EQUIPPED WITH:
GOOD EARS, BANDAIDS,
NAIL POLISH *for extra sparkle,*
ABSORBENT SHOULDERS,
TISSUE *(the kind that's kind to your nose),*
PATIENCE FOR THE ROUGH SPOTS,

and an encyclopedia of reasons why
I'm glad you're my friend

I know you don't feel pretty
even though you are

But it wasn't your beauty
    that found room in my heart

{ WE COVER OUR
FRECKLES
AND HIDE OUR THIGHS,
WE DYE OUR HAIR
AND SHADOW OUR EYES, }

WE FEEL TOO SOMETHING, NOT ENOUGH SOMETHING ELSE...

AND WE THINK, *"Am I okay, am I enough?"*

LOUDER THAN LIFE,

THE *God* OF BEAUTY SINGS,

"YES!"

YOU —

irreplaceable

kind   simple

passionate

blessed

loved

precious

oNe – of – A – KiNd

AccEPTeD

RARe

COmPLeX

COLORful

BeaUTifuL

A RefLectiON of DiViNe CReaTiViTY

— ME

The Lord your God is with you, he is mighty to save.
He takes great delight in you, he will quiet you with his love,
he rejoices over you with singing.

ZEPHANIAH 3:17, PARAPHRASED

WHEN GOD SINGS,
I wonder what it sounds like.

Does He **ROAR** like Pavarotti

or **CROON** like Nat King Cole

or **RAISE THE ROOF** like a spirited gospel choir

or **WHISPER** a mother's lullaby?

Either way . . .

or every way . . .

God sings BECAUSE YOU GIVE HIM JOY.

The You I Know

Can tell the real from the fake
but knows when to keep it to yourself

Forgets names
but never forgets a kindness

Understands when the diet is on
and even better when it is off

Shops both smart and impulsively,
sometimes at the same time

Dreams of a future with meaning and simplicity,
where a picket fence would do just fine

Dear Friend,
Please don't feel like you're alone
There is someone who is praying

praying for your peace of mind
Hoping joy is what you find

{abstract definition of joy}

SUDDENLY,

IT BECAME SO *bright,*

SO CLEAR

—gleaming LIKE WHITE SAND—

THAT THE OUTSIDE MATTERED LESS

[*and the inside matters more*]

{ THE SOUL }

CAN SPLIT THE SKY IN TWO
AND LET THE FACE OF GOD
SHINE THROUGH...

EDNA ST. VINCENT MILLAY

Nothing is beyond God.
He shines into our darkest places
and brings to light
the mystery of Himself, living there.

AT 3:15 THIS MORNING, I sat up in bed, half awake in my dream because there you were laughing so hard, tears were streaming down your face, and you couldn't stop.

❋   ❋   ❋

You had fallen on the floor, trying to catch your breath, and when I fell back onto my pillow, happy in the thought of your joyful tears, I was sure that I heard you snort. One of those "I can't help myself" snorts that comes when you've lost all control. After snorting, there's only one thing left to do . . . change your pants. IT WAS SUCH A GREAT DREAM. When the alarm clock rang at 7:05, I welcomed the new day.

I know you don't feel weak
even though you are

But it wasn't your strength
that found room in my heart

IF TRUE BEAUTY
BLOOMS FAR BELOW THE SKIN,
REAL STRENGTH
LIVES DEEPER THAN IN MUSCLE AND BONE.

real strength rests in the reality
of who God made us to be

we are frail, we are fearfully and wonderfully made,

forged in the fires of human passion,

choking on the fumes of selfish rage,

and with these our hells and our heavens so few inches apart,

we must be awfully small,

and not as strong as we think we are

FROM RICH MULLINS' "WE ARE NOT AS STRONG AS WE THINK WE ARE"

And God says . . .

"MY GRACE IS ENOUGH;
it's all you need.
MY STRENGTH
comes into its own
IN YOUR WEAKNESS."

2 CORINTHIANS 12:9

FROM *THE MESSAGE*

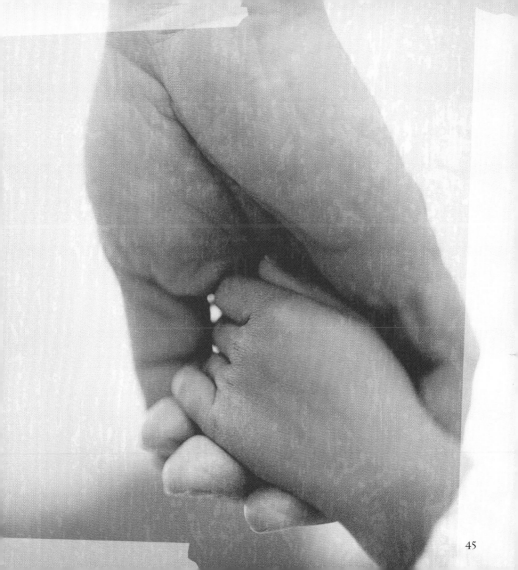

WE WERE NOT MEANT TO
HOLD ON FOR THE RIDE.
WE WERE MEANT TO LET GO...

AND SOAR.

These words reflect the fact that however much we love each other as friends, God feels even more deeply for us. He loves us unconditionally, even when we don't deserve it. Even when we forget how much we mean to Him or how much we need Him.

Dear Child, You're in my arms
I know that you feel swept aside
but you don't have to run and hide
I chose you as my beloved daughter

I FORMED YOU, FLOATING
IN YOUR MOTHER'S WOMB,
AND I KNEW THEN
THE PERSON YOU'D BE NOW—
AND I LOVED YOU EVEN MORE
BECAUSE I KNEW.

JEREMIAH 1:3, PARAPHRASED

{ AS THE BELOVED, *the one singled out* }
{ *As the object of* GOD'S AFFECTION, }

YOU

ARE THE LITTLE GIRL

HE CHERISHES.

YOU ARE NOT LEFT STANDING BY THE FENCE
WHILE THE OTHERS RUN TO PLAY

YOU WERE CHOSEN

CLUMSY,
OUTSPOKEN,
GRACEFUL,
SHY,
LAUGHING,
TEAR-STAINED,
SHAMEFUL,
HAPPY,
SELF-CONSCIOUS,
FULL OF PRIDE

...You *are* CHOSEN.

Hold your head up.

THE STORY
BEHIND THE SONG

THE FRIENDSHIP OF
STACIE ORRICO and
SONYA VECCHIARELLI

STACIE:

The summer before fourth grade, my family moved from Seattle to Denver. New city, new neighborhood, new house—I felt so far away from home. The first day of school was especially lonely. I sat quietly in class, halfway hoping not to be noticed, halfway hoping I would find just one friendly face. When the teacher called on a pretty little brown-haired girl to run an errand for her, the teacher told the girl she could pick a partner to go with her. The girl looked around the room, smiled the biggest smile, and pointed straight at me. Her name was Sonya.

From that day on, Sonya and I were inseparable. Like matching socks, that never get lost in the dryer. We had this instant bond, the kind of soul connection people don't think nine year olds can have (but they do). We played with our hair, flirted with boys and had our little inside jokes, like all girls do. Most of all, we laughed . . . hard and often, rolling around on the floor til our sides hurt.

Then one summer, I spent a couple of months away. When I came home, I found that Sonya was very sick. She hadn't had the strength or the courage to talk to me about it, but from her mother, I learned Sonya was suffering from anorexia nervosa. She had lost a lot of weight, but anorexia is so much more than a physical thing. She was so tired, emotionally exhausted and depressed.

It was hard for me to understand what Sonya was going through. I felt extremely helpless, and even guilty for not recognizing her illness before and for not knowing how to help her. One day, after praying for Sonya with another friend, I went home and wrote what I had not been able to say. "Dear Friend" was the only way I knew how to tell her how much she is loved, how much she is worth and how precious she is . . . to me and to God.

SONYA:

I cried the first time Stacie played "Dear Friend" for me. To have a friend that would write something so beautiful was amazing. But for her to have the strength to sing it for me, at that low point in my life, was really touching.

> When I was the sickest, I never wanted to admit that I was weak, that I couldn't do normal things. Stacie knew me so well when she wrote the line that says "I know you don't feel weak even though you are / But it wasn't your strength that found room in my heart."

❧ ❧ ❧

There have been so many times during my sickness when Stacie was there for me. When I couldn't go out, she chose to stay home with me and make sure I ate everything I had to. She always tried to encourage me, and even when it was hard to be with me, she was so patient and kind.

I have struggled with anorexia for two years now. I have bad days and good days, and I see a therapist on a weekly basis. Sometimes I still ask, "Why me?" Overall, you just have to think ahead and remember that God has a plan. I know there's more to life than this. I have my whole life ahead of me, and so I try to think about the positive things and all that God has given me. Like my family, my horses, and my Stacie.

STACIE:

Actually, in all of this, it was Sonya who taught me what it means to be a true friend. She was so patient with me. She trusted me with her pain, and she was honest with me. I was so honored to be the one she'd let be there when she cried. As much as I thought I was trying to learn how to take care of Sonya, Sonya was learning how to take care of me.

That's how it is with us. We bring out the best in each other, we pray for each other, and we believe the best for each other, in laughter or in pain. Even if weeks pass without seeing each other, when we need to remember why we love each other, a reminder is as close as the phone.

Our prayer for this book is that it will encourage others to say what they feel when they can't find the words—a small way to reach out to a friend in pain.

GOD BLESS YOU ALL!

Stacie Quico

Tonya Vecchiarutti